G

FACTOR

8 Secrets to Increasing Your Gravitational Pull at Work

G
FACTOR

*8 Secrets to Increasing Your
Gravitational Pull at Work*

JEANNETTE GRACE

MILL CITY PRESS, INC.

Mill City Press, Inc.
2301 Lucien Way #415
Maitland, FL 32751
407.339.4217
www.millcitypress.net

Printed in the United States of America.

ISBN-13: 9781635056167

TABLE OF CONTENTS

ACKNOWLEDGEMENTS

MANY OF THE NAMES of people in my G Factor group of gurus are not written on the pages of this book, but I am, without any reservation, a product of the many people in my life who have G Factor. I am thankful.

Specifically, I thank my partner in crime, Rick, for his incredible support and belief in me and what I do. You are an amazing example of Generosity G Factor. Your kindness and concern extends not only to the people one would expect you to love, like your family, but you fully give of yourself to so many. You extend your heart to those you pass by unexpectedly: offering a hot cup of coffee and a conversation, communicating "you matter." You humble me.

I thank my father, Al, for teaching me perseverance and tenacity. You are the epitome of Good-humored G Factor. You live your life with laughter and most certainly don't take yourself too seriously. I can only hope I am as spirited as you when I am in my seventies. (By the way, I blame you for my ridiculous sense of humor.)

To the person I have always told will be my greatest accomplishment—my daughter, Ariana. You make me proud, and I learn from your Genius G Factor. Your quest for depth of understanding of your faith and the awesome responsibility of teaching young minds represents your talent and intelligence. I love you infinitely, Pants.

And to all of those I haven't listed, thank you one thousand times over for blessing my life with your love, friendship, and sheer awesomeness.

INTRODUCTION

I'VE ALWAYS BEEN A people person. I like to talk with strangers in strange places, public places, food places, concert places—anywhere and everywhere. I seek out life stories and try to uncover and understand why people do what they do, say what they say, believe what they believe, and think what they think. Simply put, people *fascinate* me and there are no two alike.

My insatiable interest in people led me to study communication and psychology and launch my own communication consulting company in 2010. I noticed throughout my career there were some people I enjoyed working with and, well ... there were others I didn't enjoy so much. I expect you can relate.

My curiosity around why we are drawn to some people at work and repelled by others began to grow. I was quite confident the reasons were deeper than just personality differences. I began to observe people in the workplace and develop theories. I knew my observations alone weren't enough. I needed expert input. So, I surveyed people throughout the United States who are like you and me. People who like working with some and not as much with others.

With input from 834 working professionals, I was able to uncover why, and those answers are in this book. But before we get to that, I want you to understand the how and who of those answers, just so you know I'm not making it up. It's totally legit.

Through an electronic survey, people answered five questions. All survey participants were voluntary and were found through social media sites such as Facebook, LinkedIn, and Twitter. Some participated after receiving an email invitation through a direct email or because they had chosen to be on my mailing list. Others received an invitation card from me because I sat by them at a coffee shop or on an airplane, stood in line next to them at a store, or because they attended a training session of mine. (Remember: I like to talk to people anywhere and everywhere.)

The five questions.

One: Are you male or female?

Male	25.3%
Female	74.7%

*one person did not answer

Two: What is your age?

17 or younger	0.2%
18-20	5.4%
21-29	14.7%
30-39	32.1%
40-49	27.2%
50-59	14.5%
60 or older	5.9%

two people did not answer

Three: How much total combined money did all members of your HOUSEHOLD earn last year?

$24,999 or less	4.4%
$25,000 to $49,999	13.8%
$50,000 to $74,999	19.2%
$75,000 to $99,999	16.3%
$100,000 to $149,999	21.8%
$150,000 to $199,999	10.8%
$200,000 and up	7.3%
Prefer not to answer	6.3%

two people did not answer

Four: Which of the following best describes your current occupation?

Administrative	7.2%
Architecture and Engineering	1.1%
Arts, Design, Entertainment, Sports, and Media	3.5%
Business and Financial Operations	6.9%
Business-to-Business Sales	3.7%
Community and Social Service	3.1%
Computer/IT	5.4%
Construction	1.4%
Education, Training, and Library	14.5%
Healthcare	13.1%
Legal	2.8%
Life, Physical, and Social Science	0.8%
Maintenance	0.5%
Management	5.7%
Restaurant	2.2%
Retail	4.8%
Transportation	0.7%
Other	22.4%

Five: In the workplace, I am drawn to people who (CHOOSE five answers): Twenty-three descriptors were listed with an additional space for survey participants to add their own descriptor. Only 2.2 percent (eighteen participants) added their own descriptor and no clear patterns emerged from these particular responses.

WHAT'S NEXT?

The following chapters will unveil the top seven G Factors as identified by the 834 survey participants, along with a bonus chapter that is critical to you growing your overall G Factor. An assessment is included in chapter one to give you an idea of where your G Factor is low and where it is high.

Tips to consider as you read this book:

1) If you want to repel your coworkers, close this book right now and toss it in the trash.

2) If you want to increase your ability to get others to gravitate to you, keep reading.

3) Explore each chapter from a thoughtful, introspective state of mind.

4) Pay attention to the definition of each G Factor to ensure a good understanding of what each is.

5) Read the *True Story. I Swear it.* section to help you think about how each G Factor plays a role in your workplace.

6) Use the *Excuses People Use* section to reflect on roadblocks that may be in the way of growing your G Factor.

7) Use the *It Ain't Just Hot Air* section to get validation of the importance and usefulness of each G Factor.

8) Reflect on *I Know Them!* by identifying people you have worked with, or work with, who possess each G Factor.

9) If, and only if, you want to grow your G Factor and get others to gravitate to you, complete and follow through with the *Growing My G Factor* plan in chapter ten.

CHAPTER ONE

What is G Factor and Do I Have It?

FOR THE PAST SEVERAL years I have toyed with the idea that each of us has the ability to repel others or, if we choose, the power to draw others to us. In other words, just like objects on the earth and in outer space, we have gravitational pull. Think about people who just seem to have "It." These are people recognized and respected by others. They are chosen to be leaders, supervisors, mentors, and role models. Instead of repelling people, they draw them in. They are the people we enjoy being around and desire to know better than many others who cross our paths. Yes. These are people with what I call **G Factor**.

G Factor: the gravitational pull a person has that draws others to them.

When we are drawn to people in the workplace, we typically:

- seek information from them.

- want to be on projects or teams with them.
- like to eat lunch with them.
- confide in them.
- ask them for opinions or advice.
- hope to work for them.
- speak positively of them to others.

When we are repelled by people in the workplace we might:

- avoid conversations with them.
- choose to sit away from them.
- act busy when they come around.
- complain to others about them.
- avoid working on projects and teams with them.
- ask to be transferred to other departments.
- not respect or follow what they recommend.
- avoid them altogether.

Maybe you have a feel for which of the two lists you fall into simply by reading them. It's possible you twitched when something on the repelled-by list hit too close to home. Or maybe you smiled meekly when something on the drawn-to list felt real. Nonetheless, the higher your G Factor is the more success you will have in your career. (Keep in mind we are all works in progress; therefore, it's perfectly okay to not be perfect. The goal is to always be growing our G Factor.)

Wondering how high your G Factor is? Let's see.

	Never	Rarely	Sometimes	Frequently	Always
1) My coworkers help me when I ask for help.	0	1	2	3	4
2) I appreciate the people I work with.	0	1	2	3	4
3) I tell my coworkers I appreciate them.	0	1	2	3	4
4) I express my appreciation in writing.	0	1	2	3	4
5) I openly give credit where it is due.	0	1	2	3	4
6) I laugh at myself.	0	1	2	3	4
7) My coworkers think I have a good sense of humor.	0	1	2	3	4
8) I am cheerful at work.	0	1	2	3	4
9) I am open to feedback, even when it isn't positive.	0	1	2	3	4
10) I make my coworkers laugh.	0	1	2	3	4
11) I check in with my coworkers to see how they are.	·0	1	2	3	4

	Never	Rarely	Sometimes	Frequently	Always
12) When a coworker is struggling, I listen.	0	1	2	3	4
13) I do nice things for the people I work with.	0	1	2	3	4
14) I help others out at work without them asking.	0	1	2	3	4
15) I care about the people I work with.	0	1	2	3	4
16) I communicate clearly and openly.	0	1	2	3	4
17) My coworkers do not see me as bossy.	0	1	2	3	4
18) I listen.	0	1	2	3	4
19) I help others solve problems themselves.	0	1	2	3	4
20) I help my coworkers grow personally and professionally.	0	1	2	3	4
21) I impact my coworkers in a positive way.	0	1	2	3	4
22) I motivate my coworkers.	0	1	2	3	4

	Never	Rarely	Sometimes	Frequently	Always
23) I am optimistic.	0	1	2	3	4
24) I treat my coworkers with respect.	0	1	2	3	4
25) I manage workplace stress well.	0	1	2	3	4
26) I know how I make my team better.	0	1	2	3	4
27) I know how I hinder my team.	0	1	2	3	4
28) My coworkers are aware of how I can best help them.	0	1	2	3	4
29) I understand and use my best skills.	0	1	2	3	4
30) I am honest if I don't have knowledge or skill for a task.	0	1	2	3	4
31) My coworkers are not afraid to tell me they messed up.	0	1	2	3	4
32) I don't expect to be perfect.	0	1	2	3	4
33) I don't expect my coworkers to be perfect.	0	1	2	3	4

	Never	Rarely	Sometimes	Frequently	Always
34) I treat mistakes as learning opportunities.	0	1	2	3	4
35) I learn as much from my failures as from my successes.	0	1	2	3	4
36) I socialize with positive, fun people at work.	0	1	2	3	4
37) I seek input from experienced coworkers.	0	1	2	3	4
38) I look for chances to work with well-respected people.	0	1	2	3	4
39) I avoid negative coworkers when possible.	0	1	2	3	4
40) I know who makes me feel good and who makes me feel bad at work.	0	1	2	3	4

GRATITUDE: Show my apprecia-tion. (1–5)

TOTAL

_____/20

GOOD-HUMORED: Laugh and don't take myself too seriously. (6–10)

TOTAL

_____/20

GENEROSITY: Show kindness and concern for others. (11–15)

TOTAL

_____/20

GUIDE: Coach instead of direct. (16–20)

TOTAL

_____/20

GENERATE: Inspire and be infectious. (21–25)

TOTAL

_____/20

GENIUS: Demonstrate talent and intelligence. (26–30)

TOTAL

_____/20

GRANT: Give people (including myself) permission to make mistakes. (31–35)

TOTAL

_____/20

GATHER: Surround myself with others who ooze G Factor. (36–40)

TOTAL

_____/20

List your G Factors in order from highest total to lowest total.

1) _____

2) _____

3) _____

4) _____

5) _____

6) _____

7) _____

8) _____

Congratulations. You now know what your strongest G Factor is.

Perhaps you will choose to go directly to the chapter for your strongest G Factor and read. Maybe you will go to the chapter for your weakest G Factor. Either way, read with an open mind and, if you really, honestly, truly, want to grow your G Factor, spend time in chapter ten and work your plan.

CHAPTER TWO

GRATITUDE:
Show my appreciation.

"The deepest craving of human nature is the need to be appreciated." William James

LET ME BEGIN WITH a little gratitude myself. Thank you. Thank you for reading this book because you care about your success. Now, let's dig in.

TRUE STORY. I SWEAR IT.

It is interesting when we become loyal to someone simply because he or she appreciates us. Enter Glenice into my life in 1994. I didn't know Glenice well at the time. I was just a college student who was also a young, single mother. Glenice was the Margaret Thatcher (minus the short temper) of our state's marketing student organization. I had heard of her. I had seen her. But I had never talked to her. She was respected and revered throughout the state not only by my college instructors, but by all the instructors who were involved in the student organization.

I never knew Glenice noticed me until a couple of years after finishing the program I was in. It was 1997 and I decided I was going to kick off my public speaking career. One of the first steps I took was to reach out to Glenice and volunteer to present at the fall student conference ... for free. I knew this would require time off from work and gas money to drive the 140 miles to the conference and the 140 miles back home, not to mention a small token of appreciation to a friend who would watch my daughter while I was out of town.

Imagine the shock I experienced when I contacted Glenice and she knew exactly who I was. She thanked me for calling her and, in no time, I was on the schedule to present. Oh. My. Goodness.

Scared, nervous, and completely unaware of my inexperience, I presented two sessions at the conference. Glenice could not have been more kind and appreciative for my contribution as an alumnus to the conference. She not only thanked me with a hug, conversation, and the actual words "thank you," she thanked me with a check. Wow. My first paid gig as a professional speaker. It was crazy. She was doing me the favor by allowing me to kick off my speaking career, yet she was thanking me.

My loyalty to Glenice grew over the almost next two decades until her retirement in 2013. In those years, she never failed to thank me with emails, notes in the mail, and face-to-face conversations. Throughout those years, when Glenice called to ask if I would take time to speak to state senators regarding the benefits and funding needs of student organizations, I said YES. When she needed me to stay late at a conference to help load the truck, I said YES. When she asked me to help at a conference her colleague oversaw, I said YES. Whether I worked without pay or for pay, when Glenice asked I said YES. I said YES because I knew she appreciated any and all I did. It was never a question. All because she had Gratitude G Factor.

EXCUSES PEOPLE USE.

The number one reason people surveyed identified being drawn to others in the workplace is because they show appreciation. In other words, people like working with people who show gratitude. It is such a simple thing to do, yet an incredible number of people in workplaces are hungry for it. This means we are not appreciating each other enough. Why is that?

Perhaps that question is meant to be rhetorical; each person would probably answer it differently. In talking with people like you and me, I have heard a variety of excuses.

> "Why should I have to tell someone thank you for showing up to work?"

Valid. My first answer is: you don't have to. My second answer is: if you want to increase your G Factor, it is a good place to begin. Think of it this way—does showing appreciation damage relationships or suck people dry of their motivation? No. Of course not. We humans are simple. We are like puppies. When we express our gratitude to a puppy for using the outdoors instead of the indoors to relieve itself, we perpetuate the desired outcome or reaction. The puppy realizes its behavior earns positive attention and, in an effort to please, will increase the frequency of relieving itself outside. Ta-da! People are similar. When we know we please our coworker, our boss, a customer, etc., we tend to perpetuate the same behavior.

> "I'm too busy to take notice of what others are doing."

Another way to say that is, "I don't have time to care." Hmmm. Well, again, it's up to you if you take the time to notice; however, if you want to increase your G Factor, it's time to take time. Let's reverse the perspective for a moment and put ourselves in the seat of a new employee. Think back to your first job. Maybe you were a dishwasher at a restaurant like me. Maybe you folded clothes at Gap or slung manure for a farmer. Maybe you did something a bit more glamorous like valet cars at a swanky establishment. In any case, chances are the person training you took notice of what you did wrong so you could become better at what you did. If they were good at training you, they caught you doing things right so you would do them again. In either situation, the feedback changed your performance and was meaningful in your becoming a valuable employee. It didn't take the trainer long to give you feedback, and he was likely eager to do it because it was part of his job as the trainer. The key to overcoming the too busy excuse is in the sentence you just read. It doesn't take long to show appreciation. Squeak sixty seconds out of your day to focus on showing appreciation to someone. If you just can't find sixty seconds anywhere, trade something else you are doing at work right now and replace it with noticing another person's great work. Then express your appreciation for it. You know, trade staring out the window and not thinking for thinking about how a coworker helped you get your job done.

"We don't have a recognition program."

So what? I say. Is it possible to show appreciation even if your company doesn't have a formalized program for doing so? Yes, it is. Don't wait for your organization to start. I doubt you will be reprimanded for showing appreciation to a coworker, so there shouldn't be any risk at all. Be the catalyst in your department or company and start showing appreciation.

IT AIN'T JUST HOT AIR.

A plethora of research can be found in positive psychology about how gratitude increases a person's well-being. So, let's begin with positive psychology. What is it? Good question.

Positive psychology is a scientific approach to understanding what human beings, communities, and organizations do to become their best. It's been around for decades but took root when Dr. Martin Seligman, commonly known as the father of positive psychology, became president of the American Psychological Association (APA) in 1998. Early in his career, Seligman noticed psychology was focused on what was wrong with people instead of what was right with people. He wanted change. Seligman wrote, "The aim of positive psychology is to begin to catalyze a change in the focus of psychology from preoccupation only with repairing

the worst things in life to also building positive quali-
ties."[1] As president of the APA, Seligman became a catalyst in the advancement of positive psychology. Today,
a seemingly unending list of researchers have con-
tinued this advancement by positing that gratitude is
an important piece of positive psychology. The research
conducted has produced a great deal of support.

First, gratitude has been credited as an influencer of
pro-social behavior. Emmons and Shelton of University
of California, Davis noted " ... gratitude has important
implications both for societal functioning and for collective well-being."[2] Second, a 2012 study by Bersin &
Associates found saying "thank you" or making employee
recognition a priority resulted in a 14 percent increase
in employee engagement and productivity. These two
studies alone help us see the link between gratitude and
the workplace. When we express gratitude at work, we
get along better, feel better, and do better too.

Let's circle back to the father of positive psychology,
Martin Seligman. Harvard Medical School highlighted
a study of Seligman's in 2011 in their Harvard Mental
Health Letter. In this study he " ... tested the impact of

[1] Martin E.P. Seligman and Mihaly Csikszentmihalyi, "Positive Psychology:
    an introduction," *American Psychologist* 55, no.1 (2000): 5–14.

[2] R.A. Emmons and C.M. Shelton, "Chapter 33," in the *Handbook
    of Positive Psychology*, ed. C.R. Snyder and Shane J. Lopez (Oxford:
    Oxford University Press, 2000), 463.

various positive psychology interventions on 411 people, each compared with a control assignment of writing about early memories. When their week's assignment was to write and personally deliver a letter of gratitude to someone who had never been properly thanked for his or her kindness, participants immediately exhibited a huge increase in happiness scores."[3] This is the bonus to expressing gratitude. The person expressing it receives even greater benefits than the person receiving it.

I KNOW THEM!

You have likely worked with, or are working with right now, people who possess Gratitude G Factor. Reflect and write those names below. Then take it one step further and identify HOW they demonstrate gratitude.

Name:

How they showed gratitude is:

Name:

How they showed gratitude is:

---

[3] www.health.harvard.edu/newsletter_article/in-praise-of-gratitude

Name:

How they showed gratitude is:

Name:

How they showed gratitude is:

Name:

How they showed gratitude is:

CHAPTER THREE

GOOD-HUMORED: Laugh and don't take myself too seriously.

"A sense of humor... is needed armor. Joy in one's heart and some laughter on one's lips is a sign that the person down deep has a pretty good grasp of life."
Hugh Sidey

TRUE STORY. I SWEAR IT.

Let me introduce you to Jeff. I began working with Jeff in 2011. We don't work together in my company, but we are what others call "business associates." Jeff works for an organization that sometimes has clients who need the services I provide. He serves as the conduit between his clients' needs and my services.

Jeff cracks me up on a regular basis. One of my favorite mediums to interact with him is via email. He uses words in a way that tickles my funny bone. If I am being completely honest, I have involuntarily let out more than one obnoxious laugh in a public place while reading his emails. Here is just a sample:

In trying to identify a student who registered under her legal name, yet goes by her middle name: "This is the kind of detective work that earns us the big bucks. ☺"

After responding to an email in which he meant to refer to a class of mine called Refresh Your Grammar and instead called it Refresh Your Grandma: Me to Jeff: "Hmmm ... I don't have a class called 'Refresh Your Grandma,' but think it would be a great topic. Are you suggesting we develop this course? I'm a little concerned Grandpas will feel left out ...."

Jeff's response: "Please do work on the Grandma class, though...I think it will be a big hit."

In the face of sickness, he still maintains his sense of humor: "I meant to email you about this last week, but I have had a crazy turn of events. I had a hacking cough that wouldn't go away plus a low-grade fever for about a week, so I finally went in to get checked out. Long story short ... I had double pneumonia and spent a fun-filled ambulance ride and weekend in the hospital. It was a laugh riot!"

And one of my most favorites was his apology for a delay in responding to another email I sent. To rectify the situation, he included a picture of himself after his attempt to be super dad. He had a large hickey on his forehead from a suction dart.

Jeff post-super dad effort.

EXCUSES PEOPLE USE.

How many people do you know who take themselves too seriously? Smiles are few and far between and laughter at work is out of the question. Perhaps the words curmudgeon, arrogant, or stick-in-the-mud come to mind. I've worked in workplaces where fun wasn't strictly prohibited, but it was certainly frowned upon.

Regardless (and this is serious business), the research shows us we are drawn to people who don't take themselves too seriously. So, what is stopping us?

"I'm just not a funny person."

Hey, that's okay. Being funny is not a requirement of not taking oneself too seriously. There are other ways to be good-humored. Take British Olympic diver Leon Taylor for example. After diving in the 1996 Atlanta games, he learned a big lesson around his level of seriousness.

> It taught me that some things are too important to take too seriously. So going into Athens the main goal was to enjoy every second of it. That didn't mean sitting back and drinking piña coladas by the Olympic Village swimming pool! It was about embracing the excitement, enjoying the bus journeys, waving at fans, interacting with other athletes, and generally being more sociable rather than walking past people because you're focused.[4]

---

[4] "'Some things are too important to take too seriously' – Leon Taylor's learnings from the Olympics." www.sportsaid.org.uk/news-main/news/some-things-are-too-important-to-take-too-seriously-leon-taylor-s-learnings-from-the-olympics/

Thanks, Leon, for the permission to let loose a little. And congratulations on your silver medal in Athens.

"We're not allowed to have fun here."

Really? What kind of a place do these people work at? If this is actually the case, guess what? The place they work at is seriously lacking Good-humored G Factor, which means they aren't attracting the best people. I think the best course of action here is to reframe what it means to be "good-humored." *Merriam-Webster Dictionary* defines it as: pleasant and cheerful. Maybe some workplaces aren't filled with birthday cakes, pizza parties, and happy hours, but it is always possible to infuse a couple pleasantries and moments of cheer when a coworker hits a deadline, a team finishes a project, or a salesperson secures an important contract.

"The work I do is serious work."

Congratulations. Maybe you are a doctor, probation officer, city administrator, vice president at a multi-national corporation. In reality, regardless of what we do, we all have parts of our work that are serious business. Why not go about it in a way that draws people to us?

Here are a couple examples of people with off-the-charts Good-humored G Factor and serious work to do as well.

First, Patch Adams. Maybe you saw the 1988 movie where Robin Williams played the doctor who found himself in trouble for being too good-humored during his medical internship, yet won the medical board over and graduated successfully. I love Hollywood. What I love even more is Hunter Doherty "Patch" Adams is a real guy. And he is a real doctor too. At age eighteen he made the choice to live every day happy. Built into the work he does is treating patients while incorporating clowning, arts and music, and play.

Second, Sir Richard Branson. A man who works hard and plays hard. A man who has never taken himself so seriously that he was afraid to fail. He communicates with the world with tweets like, "When I got knighted I did wonder whether the royal sword would be used to chop my head off" (August 12, 2016). Or the tweet that led to an article chronicling Branson boarding a Virgin flight (his own airline by the way) with twelve rolls of toilet paper and a master plan: the first row to unravel a roll of toilet paper by passing it over each person's head from the front of the plane to the back of the plane without breaking the stream, won. Ridiculous AND awesome. (Author's note: if he wasn't so happily married and I wasn't happily with my man since 2009, I would seriously consider a move to England.)

IT AIN'T JUST HOT AIR.

Laughter is good. Laughter is a way for us to express joy and happiness, not to mention amusement. Although laughter is a physical response to some sort of stimulus, it is powerfully positive and can affect others in a powerfully positive way as well. "The psychological effects of laughter relate primarily to both its use as a coping mechanism and ... its enhancement of interpersonal relationships."[5] Well, it seems like that pretty much sums up how laughter is part of Good-humored G Factor.

Cheerfulness promotes productivity. A 700-person study conducted in 2015 showed happy employees are approximately 12 percent more productive because employees who are happy make more of an effort. The research found "a causal link between human well-being and human performance."[6] This goes to say, we gravitate to the coworker who gets stuff done, and cheerfulness is a way to create gravitational pull.

---

[5] J. Yim, "Therapeutic Benefits of Laughter in Mental Health: A Theoretical Review," *The Tohoku Journal of Experimental Medicine* 239, no. 3 (2016): 243–249.

[6] Daniel Sgroi. "Happiness and Productivity: Understanding the happy-productive worker." Global Perspectives Series: Paper 4 (2015).

Openness expands. No one wholeheartedly relishes being criticized. I mean, come on. Who wants to be told they didn't meet expectations? Although there is truth in the importance of delivering a message of criticism to someone at the right time and with the right words, we have less power in how messages are given to us versus how we receive them. Did you catch that? We have *more power* in how we receive a message compared to giving a message. So, first think like this—it ISN'T about ME. The purpose of feedback in almost every single case is not to make someone feel like a terrible, useless, mess of a person. The purpose is to discuss growth and change. If you take yourself so seriously that someone's perspective is devastating or, on the flip side, is rejected, you have lost perspective of how much power you have. Second, it's not the end of the world. "The key to responding in an open and constructive way is to acknowledge that you could learn from the feedback, be it positive or developmental feedback."[7] So, seriously, stop taking yourself so seriously.

I KNOW THEM!

There are people you work with right now, or worked with, who seem to bring joy to a room because they have Good-humored G Factor and don't take themselves too seriously. Who are those people? Brainstorm their

---

[7] University of South Australia (2012) Providing Quality Feedback: A good practice guide. People Development and Performance.

names and then identify HOW they showed they were good-humored.

    Name:

        How they showed they were good-humored is:

    Name:

        How they showed they were good-humored is:

    Name:

        How they showed they were good-humored is:

    Name:

        How they showed they were good-humored is:

    Name:

        How they showed they were good-humored is:

CHAPTER FOUR

GENEROSITY:
Show kindness and
concern for others.

"It takes generosity to discover the whole through others. If you realize you are only a violin, you can open yourself up to the world by playing your role in the concert." Jacques Cousteau

TRUE STORY. I SWEAR IT.

This person requires me to go back a couple decades (okay, almost three decades) to the beginning of my career. Let me clarify something before launching into who this person is. I have worked with many people who showed generosity. People who checked in on me if I was having a tough day. People who signed an enormous poster with loving sentiments and then hung it on my office door after my mom passed away. People who picked up the slack when I was overwhelmed. I appreciate every one of their actions of generosity, but Diane made an impression on me that has stuck with me my entire career—her Generosity G Factor was that profound.

I met Diane when I was eighteen years old. She was married with two children close to my age. Diane managed an optometric office where I was hired as a part-time frame consultant. My job was to help patients choose the perfect frame for their eyeglasses ... and learn from Diane. About six months after working with her, I found myself pregnant at the just-recently-turned age of nineteen. I gave birth to my daughter and was raising her as not only the sole parent, but also as the sole provider. During this time, Diane decided she wanted less stress and fewer work hours, so I was hired as the full-time office manager. I was now Diane's boss and a naïve and inexperienced manager. Looking back, I must note her patience with me was outstanding.

What makes Diane's Generosity G Factor so profound is that it was always understated. It wasn't self-serving or recognition-seeking in any way. She knew supporting my daughter was challenging emotionally at times and extremely difficult financially. Although I never told her, she probably figured out how financially difficult it was for me when she saw me wear the same few outfits day after day, for two straight years. I just didn't have money to buy myself anything I did not absolutely need. She knew I shared a room with my daughter, lived with two roommates in a two-bed-room apartment, and drove a car with an oil leak. Her intuition maybe told her I watched TV in the dark so I could save money on the electric bill. She never made me feel ashamed, embarrassed, or less than. What Diane did was find secret opportunities to help me. When her mother-in-law passed away she made it seem as if I would be doing her a huge favor if I was to take the pots and pans (I had no idea how high-end they were), kitchen utensils, and plastic Christmas tree with every required accoutrement. I mean, after all, they would have to figure out what organization would accept it as a donation or they would just have to throw it out. Or so she made it sound. Diane was also an amazing cook. She made delicious Italian food that made my mouth water. Often, she would arrive at work and say, "Oh, I made too much last night and Jerry and I didn't eat it all. I don't want to throw it out." I would happily accept it, knowing my refrigerator had what my daughter needed, but I faced eating buttered noodles ... again. Never once, until years later, did it occur to me Diane and Jerry probably didn't just happen to frequently have "extra" food—she was too good a cook to overestimate portions that much.

Thank you, Diane, for your Generosity G Factor.

EXCUSES PEOPLE USE.

It is possible generosity comes easier to some than others. You see, our workplaces are made up of people who are more task-focused or more people-focused. (You probably have an idea of which side you fall on.) Generally, those who are people-focused are more attuned to how people are feeling and doing compared to those who are task-focused. Their intuition might give them a clue something is wrong with a coworker, or they may just simply be wondering how a coworker is doing. Those who are task-focused are just that: focused on the work. It isn't that task-focused people are jerks and don't have feelings or don't care about their coworkers, it's just their attention is naturally drawn to the work. Regardless of your inclination to be people- or task-focused, you might use some of these excuses.

> "I am kind to others, but they don't seem
> to do the same."

G Factor isn't about reciprocity and shouldn't be dependent on others' actions. The whole idea of this book is to help you build *your* G Factor. If you wait for others to be kind and show concern first, your G Factor will wither away. It will shrivel up like a raisin in the sun. Take a moment to honestly answer this question: Am I feeling sorry for myself?

"Work is about work."

From the point of view of the person who owns or runs your organization, I agree. You are at work to do a job. However, we are dynamic, not static, human beings. This means that when we come to work we are not robots who have left all needs of humanness and belonging at home. Showing kindness and concern to others can be about task. For example, if I know an unexpected meeting is going to demand all your attention and require last-minute copies of a report, I can offer to make the copies for you so you can focus on getting your thoughts together before the meeting begins.

"I don't have time to even think about it."

This is completely and utterly fine if you don't want to increase your G Factor. If you do want to increase your G Factor, throw this excuse out the window with any others in your repertoire of lame excuses.

"I've got my own problems to take care of."

This is precisely why we need to practice Generosity G Factor. Human nature is fascinating because when we change our behavior, people usually respond in a way that matches our behavior. Is this always true? No. But the odds are in your favor. Take, for example, a negative interaction. If one person raises her voice, the other person will likely raise his voice in return. Now, let's look at a positive interaction. If you smile and say good morning, you are likely to get a smile and a good morning right back.

If you feel your problems are preventing you from showing kindness and concern to others, you may be headed for burnout. So, the lesson is this: if we show kindness and concern for others when they are overwhelmed, they will likely do the same for us. This unexpected reciprocity reduces our stress and likelihood of burnout at the same time.

IT AIN'T JUST HOT AIR.

I know this idea of generosity is a little touchy-feely for some, but the benefits received when we show kindness and concern for others is backed up with science.

Author David Hamilton, PhD, identified *The 5 Side Effects of Kindness.*

1. Kindness Makes Us Happier.
2. Kindness Gives Us Healthier Hearts.

3. Kindness Slows Ageing.
4. Kindness Makes for Better Relationships.
5. Kindness is Contagious.[8]

Dr. Hamilton explained how kindness impacts our bodies on a biochemical level. When we do nice things for others, we elevate the dopamine in our brain, which produces a natural high. Our bodies also produce oxytocin, which is known to expand the blood vessels in our heart, and in turn positively impact ageing. Bonus.

In Kelly McGonigal's 2013 TedTalk, she cites a study that "tracked about 1,000 adults in the United States, and they ranged in age from 34 to 93 .... People who spent time caring for others showed absolutely no stress-related increase in dying. Zero. Caring created resilience."[9]

If these benefits aren't enough to encourage you to increase your Generosity G Factor, try this one.

In the past decade, considerable research on pro social motivation in the workplace has been conducted. To bring context to what you are about to read, let's use

---

[8] "The 5 Side Effects of Kindness," David R Hamilton, last revised May 30, 2011, www.drdavidhamilton.com/the-5-side-effects-of-kindness.

[9] Kelly McGonigal, "How to Make Stress Your Friend," TedTalks (lecture series), (2013). www.ted.com/talks/kelly_mcgonigal_how_to_make_stress_your_friend [citing: Michael J. Poulin et al. (2013) Giving to Others and The Association Between Stress and Mortality. *American Journal of Public Health*.]

Spritzer and Cameron's definition of pro social motivation: the ability to "take initiative, persist in meaningful tasks, help others, enhance the well-being of others, strengthen cooperation and collaboration ...."[10] In other words, when pro social motivation is present, employees are more inspired, proactive, creative, better performing, and more energetic. More specifically, in a 2015 study "'team members' shared desire to focus on benefitting others."[11] This study included participants from eighty-four work teams (474 individuals) in the United States and China and 496 undergraduate business students from a university in the Midwest of the United States. The evidence showed kindness and caring positively impacts both team processes and effectiveness. It just might be fair to say Generosity G Factor "may bring about smoother interactions and more effective cooperation ...."[11]

I KNOW THEM!

Think of the people you work with now, or worked with, who touched your heart and made you feel cared

[10] Kim S. Cameron and Gretchen M. Spreitzer, eds., *The Oxford Handbook of Positive Organizational Scholarship* (Oxford: Oxford University Press, 2011).

[11] J. Hu & R.C. Liden. (2015) "Making a Difference in the Teamwork: Linking Team Prosocial Motivation to Team Processes and Effectiveness," *Academy of Management Journal* 58, no. 4 (2015): 1102–1127.

about. These are the people who possess Generosity G Factor. Write their names below and take time to identify how they showed their generosity.

Name:

How they showed generosity is:

Name:

How they showed generosity is:

Name:

How they showed generosity is:

Name:

How they showed generosity is:

Name:

How they showed generosity is:

CHAPTER FIVE

GUIDE:
Coach instead of direct.

"Coaching takes you from where you are right now (regardless of the past) and helps you move toward where you want to be." Michelle Stimpson

TRUE STORY. I SWEAR IT.

What is a coach? *Merriam-Webster Dictionary* defines it as: "one who instructs or trains." *The Cambridge Dictionary* uses: "an expert who trains someone learning or improving a skill, esp. one related to performing." *Macmillan Dictionary* states: "someone who teaches a special skill, especially one connected with performing such as singing or acting."

A singer or actress I am not. However, after owning my business for a couple years I recognized I needed help to take it to the proverbial next level. A coach. So,

I began searching for help. Not just any help, but professional help. I found career coaches, leadership coaches, life coaches, and many other types of coaches. I was looking for something specific. I wanted someone who understood what it was like to be an entrepreneur or, as some call it, a solopreneur. But they needed business savvy, marketing knowledge, and a fun-loving personality too. Not too much to ask for, right?

I also needed someone who understood the act of coaching.

Coaching, defined as an ongoing approach to managing people:

- creates a genuinely motivating climate for performance
- improves the match between an employee's actual performance and expected performance
- increases the probability of an employee's success by providing timely feedback, recognition, clarity, and support

Enter Amy, a business coach. It might seem like a no-brainer that I tell a story here about a business "coach." After all, Guide G Factor is about coaching instead of directing. *Warning!* Sometimes things are not as they seem.

The truth is, working with Amy was a painful process. Not difficult. Not challenging. Not uncomfortable. Painful. Amy had me doing the work, the thinking, the digging in, the heavy lifting. At first I thought, "Hey, didn't I hire you to figure this out for me?" No was the answer. I soon learned that although Amy could tell me what to do and how to do it, it was in fact *not* what I hired her to do. She was improving my actual performance so I could achieve my desired performance.

Amy couldn't define my ideal client. I needed to be the person to identify the type of people and organizations I felt most excited to work with. She couldn't decide what topics I wanted to focus on in an effort to stop trying to be all things to all organizations. I had to figure out in what areas of expertise I believed I could truly offer my clients exceptional help. My business coach couldn't tell me what my pricing structure should be. She could, however, ask the right questions to uncover why I was donating my knowledge and experience in some cases without even knowing it. She was increasing my likelihood of success by helping me clarify ideal clients, topics, and passion points.

When I veered off my plan, Amy never scolded me or told me I was off track. Instead, she reminded me of where I said I wanted to be. When I became overwhelmed with running a business, Amy didn't tell me

I needed to follow through on my goals. Alternatively, she supported me and made herself available when I was finally able to do the work. In essence, Amy created a climate that motivated me to be better at what I did and how I did it.

From my business coach I learned to think deeply, sideways, backways, and in all directions to discover what I wanted my business to be and then take the necessary steps to make it happen. The result? I increased my value to my clients, my business doubled in less than two years, and each day I get closer and closer to my goal of playing more than I work. Yay for me. And thanks to Amy for having Guide G Factor.

EXCUSES PEOPLE USE.

Oh, resisting the impulse of telling someone what to do, how to do it, and when to do it is a hard thing to do. Every person is an expert in something and when a situation arises and that expertise is needed, it can be so so so difficult not to jump in and take charge. The problem with telling instead of coaching is we teach people to have others do the thinking for them. It is the antithesis of coaching, and yet we make excuses that sometimes sound like these.

> "I have too much to do to and sometimes people just need to be told so it can get done."

I won't disagree with that line of thinking. There are times when coaching isn't the answer. On the flipside, there are times when coaching *is* the answer and taking time to do it has long-term payoffs. If a person never has time to coach and only has time to direct, chances are the problem isn't the situation itself. Looking deeper might unveil something difficult to accept about oneself, but it will also be meaningful and a step in overcoming an excuse to lack Guide G Factor.

> "Some people can't be coached."

Oh, come on! I have been known to view the world from a perspective of grey (there is always a way, a solution, an answer, etc.), but if we don't believe in people's ability to grow and change, where are we? A workplace where no one invests in your development is not a workplace that retains good people. This reminds me of a story in one of the books that lives in my personal resource library. "Reportedly, IBM's Thomas J. Watson was asked if he was going to fire an employee who made a mistake that cost IBM $600,000. He said, 'No, I just spent $600,000 training him. Why would I want somebody else to hire his experience?'"[12] Enough said.

> "There are some things in the workplace
> that must be directed."

At face value this is true. For example, safety is something that needs to be directed in the moment. If you have a coworker or employee conducting him or herself in a way that puts others or the organization at risk, it needs to be dealt with immediately and oftentimes head-on in a non-negotiable manner. Sort of like a toddler who reaches for a hot stove. To prevent large-scale damage, we direct. There is the afterward we still need to consider; what can be done after the fact to coach someone to make safer or better choices in the future? How can motivation be created or uncovered that encourages an employee to make safe choices going forward?

IT AIN'T JUST HOT AIR.

Perhaps the reason so many people prefer to be coached, opposed to directed, is it feels respectful. A person's intelligence is acknowledged while, at the same time, their skill set is honed. Let's look at coaching in

---

[12] Joe Griffith, *Speaker's Library of Stories, Anecdotes and Humor* (Englewood Cliffs: Prentice Hall, 1990), 115.

the workplace from two perspectives: peer-to-peer and leader-to-follower.

A simple definition of peer-to-peer coaching is: to help our coworkers grow professionally. It supports the adage we can do more together than we can do alone. It is an opportunity available to all of us; however, successfully doing it requires deeper understanding. Let's get deeper then.

In a 2008 study by Parker, Hall, and Kram, participants reported multiple positive results of peer-to-peer coaching including:

- Success in dealing with change
- Support for personal and professional goals
- Increased confidence
- Improved accuracy on self-image
- Development of "soft" skills
- Fostering empowerment
- Improved delivery of feedback[13]

This means peer-to-peer coaching improves how individuals view themselves and in turn positively impacts their work contributions.

---

[13] Polly Parker, Douglas T. Hall, and Kathy E. Kram, "Peer Coaching: A Relational Process for Accelerating Career Learning," *Academy of Management Learning & Education* 7, no. 4 (2008): 487–503.

Although peer coaching has deep roots and years of research in the education arena, research supporting its impact in the workplace is just beginning to grow legs, and the legs are promising. Specifically, the afore-mentioned study by Parker, Hall, and Kram concluded that many of the students who participated in the study were also executives in the workplace and were likely applying the same coaching processes.

To further support this point, agility expert, author, and speaker Mike Richardson worked heavily with peer groups in small to medium-sized businesses and wit-nessed the advantages of peer-to-peer work in teams. In 2010 he wrote, "I never cease to be amazed at the creative problem solving, issue resolution and innova-tion which routinely arises from these groups (and, not least of all, management innovation) because of the high functionality of the trust, transparency and dia-log."[14] Richardson's sentiments show us peer-to-peer coaching has a notable impact on workplace success of individuals, teams, and possibly the organization as a whole. This notion is supported by others such as author James Surowiecki who believes in collective intelligence and that a group's ability to problem solve is better than an individual's ability to problem solve. Perhaps it is

---

[14] www.managementexchange.com/story/power-peer-group-how-come-something-so-proven-not-more-pervasive-and-what-are-we-willing-do-ab

best summarized by author Mila N. Baker's words in 2014 when she wrote, "It is a shift to a model where knowledge and intelligence is distributed throughout the organization from the periphery of the system to the center of the system—a shift that allows us to look at a more integrative model between individuals, work units, and the organization."[15] In other words, allowing peers to concentrate on their talents and strengths by coaching others to use theirs produces a better outcome.

So, although the research on peer-to-peer coaching is relatively young, I speculate its impact is considerable given those surveyed for this book rated it as the fourth highest reason they are drawn to others in the workplace.

Now, let's look at coaching from the leader-to-follower perspective.

BlessingWhite, a global leadership development and employee engagement consulting firm, released a research report in 2016 including input from 3,700 managers and their direct reports. Seventy-nine percent of managers like to coach, and, even more importantly, 80 percent of employees want to be coached. The research also revealed a match in importance of the top

---

[15] Mila N. Baker, *Peer to Peer Leadership: Why the Network is the Leader* (San Francisco: Berrett-Koehler Publishers, Inc., 2013) 12.

three coaching behaviors that were most beneficial in the eyes of the leader AND the follower.

1. Communicating clearly and candidly.
2. Establishing clear objectives and milestones.
3. Delivering on promises made.[16]

However, there is a problem. Many leaders may not be coaching, according to ForbesCustom.com. Forbes highlighted a 2011 study by Bersin & Associates in their article "Research Shows Impact of Senior Leaders Who Coach and Develop Employees" where 70 percent of organizations think they are coaching their employees, yet only 11 percent of senior leaders were performing daily coaching. These senior leaders are missing out on Guide G Factor.

The question may still remain in your head, "How is coaching beneficial?"

Take, for example, Dr. Steve Nguyen and the multiple benefits to coaching he identified such as: easier to delegate tasks, increased productivity, less time dealing with performance issues, employee retention, employees use new skills for career advancement, and employee pride and satisfaction.

---

[16] "The Coaching Conundrum: Coaching in the post-performance-assessment era". (2016). Blessing White. A Division of GP Strategies. p. 7.

Returning to Bersin & Associates' study, they found stronger business results can be enjoyed up to a whopping 130 percent when managers are trained to coach and do coach and 21 percent when senior leaders do it. Additionally, employee engagement, productivity, and customer service increases 39 percent. For example, you have a salesperson who is doing a great job meeting the company's sales goal of one million dollars per year. Based on past performance, you know this employee needs little assistance to perform well; however, they express a desire to grow new business. Together, you develop a plan on how to prospect within a new industry. In eighteen-months the salesperson increases sales to $2,300,000 (130 percent). So, the ongoing development of followers—such as helping them identify how they are going to get from where they are to where they want to be—can produce great rewards for an organization, a leader, and a follower. Wow. If you were still wondering how coaching can be beneficial a few minutes ago, I think your brain can rest now.

I KNOW THEM!

Take a moment first to reflect on the people you have worked with who had equal power as you AND have Guide G Factor.

A time when a coworker *challenged my way of thinking or problem solving.*

    Name:

        How they guided was:

A time when a coworker *helped me learn a new skill, process, etc.*

    Name:

        How they guided was:

A time when a coworker and I *helped each other grow.*

    Name:

        How they guided was:

Take a moment first to reflect on the people who have supervised you AND have Guide G Factor.

A supervisor who *listened to me and cared about what I said.*

Name:

How they guided was:

A supervisor who *let me find and use my own path to produce a result.*

Name:

How they guided was:

A supervisor who *taught me the importance of accountability.*

Name:

How they guided was:

CHAPTER SIX

GENERATE:
Inspire and be infectious.

"If your actions inspire others to dream more, learn more, do more and become more, you are a leader."
John Quincy Adams

TRUE STORY. I SWEAR IT.

Smiles. Positivity. Vision. High energy. Intelligence. Zest for life. Lover of personal and professional growth. Over and over again I have seen my friend Jessica, or Jess as I call her, inspire people with these amazingly infectious ways of working. Let's go back to 2003 when we began working together as instructors in a business program at a technical college. I didn't know much about her prior to beginning my job at the college, but I did know of her. She had a reputation ... a positive one that is. Even her black hair, Snow White-like skin, and red lips preceded her.

At first, Jess was a little apprehensive about getting to know me. Why? She had been burned before by a coworker (a long story we won't get into because it is full of the antithesis of G Factor). I had a couple personality traits that reminded her of this previous coworker. As I earned her trust with my own G Factor, I began to understand hers.

Students most definitely gravitated to Jess. It was commonplace to hear them tout her teaching ability or share the myriad of reasons they liked her classes. Success story after success story of Jess's ability to inspire people to do better than they thought they could would require a larger number of pages than planned for this chapter and this book. So, I decided I would go to Jessica and ask her what she believes she did to generate, or inspire and be infectious? Knowing she is hard on herself, I knew this would be a great exercise to get her to recognize her own G Factor. This is what she wrote:

> I feel most inspiring when I am walking in the most daring version of my authentic self. When I take personal risks of some sort. When I am outside my comfort zone, and I invest myself in what I am doing with less care about

"how I am coming off." I think the key to inspiring people is letting them know you care. When I was a teacher and saw unique or raw talent I would try to make sure students knew they had something special. There are so many ways teachers have the opportunity to do this. I know I missed opportunities to do this, and I feel bad about students who passed through my classroom and never knew they had something special because I never said or did something to ensure they heard it from me. But for the ones for whom it "worked" I think it was a mixture of "push and support" in different proportions for each person. For the students below I am confident that I could say I "inspired" them because of the evidence I have either seen or heard directly from them.

Case in point 1.

Jazzie—I know I had an effect on Jazzie because she blames me for understanding work does not just need to be a means to an end. Before our relationship she didn't know work could be more than a pay-check that allows life to happen outside of work. Because of our relationship she now believes work should be fulfilling in and of itself, and work is a place where you should let your strengths shine.

Case in point 2.

Mike—After multiple attempts to talk Mike into participating in DECA competition [student organization for business students], which included a call to his mom so she knew she should encourage him, I gave up on trying to persuade him. Soon after I gave up he was being difficult during a role-play in a class. In an act of exasperation, I wrote some coaching feedback on a note. It was my attempt to get him to "shut up." The note included positive feedback plus one "to work on." I don't remember exactly what I wrote on the note but one of the positives was something like: Able to articulate own point of view and influence others to share that point of view.

(I was pissed he was negatively affecting attitudes in the class.)

His "to work on" was: Refusal to try new things that could lead to personal and professional growth.

I didn't expect a response from Mike other than an apology for the way he was acting during class. Instead, after class he sheepishly walked up to me and said, "Sign me up." I was astounded. I asked him why he had changed his mind. He said, "Because you were right." He was referring to what I had written in the note.

Case in point 3.

Tammy—Tammy wrote a leadership-style paper about me. She also has repeatedly told me she feels "'healthier' after talking to me."

When I read this I wasn't sure what it meant, so I asked Jess about it. She shared that Tammy has explained when she and Jess have conversations, she feels a sense of centeredness and is better able to decide what is important in life.

Case in point 4.

Me. From the moment I began working with Jess I wanted to be more like her. I knew she had something special, plain and simple. I liked being around her because it felt positive and good. I found myself trying to emulate her energy in the classroom so my students would learn and be entertained at the same time just as they were in her class. I wanted to master the subjects I was teaching, just as she had. I noticed she could detect undiscovered talents in students and soon they would be competing in business competitions and taking home national first place medals in marketing events. When she gave students feedback, it was always said or written in a way that kept a student's confidence intact, yet gave them motivation to work to the next level. She dedicated herself to developing students as leaders by advising a student organization officer team. She was extremely enthusiastic about what she did, how she did it, and encouraging student growth. Her ability to generate has generated endless wedding invitations, birth announcements, requests for recommendations, and coffee get-togethers with students long after they graduated.

As I watched Jess and learned from her, I grew and became a better teacher. Working together became a source of great emotional rewards. So much so that when I was no longer teaching at the college we began a happiness movement where we did random acts of kindness for 365 days and blogged about it ... but that's a story for another book. Right now, I raise my glass to Jess's Generate G Factor.

EXCUSES PEOPLE USE.

The secret formula to Generate G Factor is ... well, there isn't a secret formula. We all inspire and are infectious; however, the trick is how to be infectious in a good way opposed to infect others like a disease. It's truly amazing how much power we have to impact those around us. There are all sorts of ridiculous excuses why a person can't inspire others. How about this one?

"There isn't anything special about me."

First, shame on the person who told you that and made you believe it too. Second, wrong. As the late author and speaker Leo Buscaglia said, "You are uniquely something that will never happen again."[17] So, take a moment to ask yourself what makes you uniquely

---

[17] Leo Buscaglia, *The Art of Being Fully Human* (Simon & Schuster, 1995) Abridged Audiobook.

you and then embrace it, own, it, celebrate it, stand in the power of it, and use it to inspire and be infectious.

"I'm not good at it."

Guess what? I don't buy that line of thinking for a second. We are constantly impacting others, and when we have awareness of how we do it, it allows us to make a choice to positively inspire and infect. Put yourself in this scenario (many have likely been in it). You're driving and realize you weren't paying enough attention to the road signs and the exit you need to take is a short distance away. Traffic is pretty heavy and you need to cross two lanes to make your exit. You put your blinker on, look over your shoulder to check your blind spot and then inch your way over. You successfully clear the first lane because a nice driver created room for you to safely maneuver over. You smile and wave and in return they smile back. Now, you need to merge into the next lane. Again, you put your blinker on to signal to other drivers you would like to move over. Your exit is getting closer and closer, and you are afraid you are going to miss it. The gap you plan to merge into suddenly gets smaller because the car in that lane speeds up. You panic. Your exit is almost on top of you. You make the decision to go for it and wedge your way across the lane and onto the exit ramp, all while hearing a blazingly loud, long, obnoxious horn. As you turn your head over your shoulder to sheepishly wave with a facial expression full of apologies, they stick their middle finger up and wave it at you. Do you want to respond to them with your middle finger? It's not a trick question, honest. If you want Generate G Factor, choosing no is the correct answer.

Here is another way of looking at excuses.

"I'm just me."

Good for you for being so humble. But what about you can give people positivity energy, hope, motivation, ideas, and so on? Figure it out. Be intentional. Let it shine.

IT AIN'T JUST HOT AIR.

If we are going to move and influence people in the workplace we must possess Generate G Factor. Let's look at it through the lens of inspirational leadership.

Inspirational leadership is a person's ability to create energy and purpose that gets others excited and moving forward. In 2016, Bain & Company tapped into 2,000 of their own employees to understand what provides inspiration for their people. The results were fascinating. The four areas identified through the research included: developing inner resources such as emotional self-awareness and stress tolerance; connecting with others through empathy, humility, shared interests, etc.; setting the tone by being open and giving credit where credit is due and owning mistakes for example; and leading the team with traits like servanthood and empowerment. To understand how inspiration impacts others in the workplace, Bain went on to determine how many traits (or defined by them as distinguishing strengths) an individual needs to possess to truly inspire others. They found, "Even one distinguishing strength nearly doubles your chances of being inspiring—and the more distinguishing strengths you have, the more inspirational you can be."[18] Remarkable.

One year previously, in 2015, Zenger Folkman, a global leadership training and coaching company, published a whitepaper on inspiring leaders and how they increased employee engagement and commitment.

> Some believe that inspiration is just something that leaders do on big occasions. They see it as that yearly speech where leaders get up in front of all the employees and get them all revved up and inspired. Inspiration is much more than this. Everything a leader does every

---

[18] www.bain.com/publications/articles/how-leaders-inspire-cracking-the-code.aspx (2016)

day has an impact on the employees. When a leader comes to work in the morning and is in a bad mood, that counts. When a leader comes in and is sharing with colleagues her optimism, excitement and passion for the work; that counts. When a leader comes in, and ducks into their office and hides in their cave all day; that counts. But if a leader will just take a few minutes to go around and ask people how they're doing, thank them and encourage them to do more; that counts. Everything leaders do counts. Everything every employee does on every level counts.[19]

The whitepaper included results from the analysis of data from 1,000 leaders who were previously ranked high as inspiring and motivating. Zenger Folkman determined what other inspiring behaviors these 1,000 leaders had. The four most common behaviors were: focused and driven to achieve organizational goals; conducted self with integrity and without compromising ethics; created a vision for the future that engages

---

[19] John H. Zenger, Joseph Folkman, and Scott Edinger, *The Inspiring Leader: Unlocking the Secret Behind How Extraordinary Leaders Motivate* (McGraw-Hill Education, 2015), 6.

people; and pulled employees in because they listened and treated them with respect. There are two other behaviors not far behind: generated energy and excitement with their passion and had the technical intelligence and experience to impact good decisions.

You may be thinking, well, I'm not a leader per se. This can be true and it's a good point. Open your mind for a moment to entertain the idea that we all lead informally in some way, which means we influence our coworkers regularly.

Employee engagement firm TINYpulse researched the reason employees disengage at work by collecting data from approximately 20,000 employees in 500 different organizations. The most common de-motivator was the lack of peer motivation or camaraderie with fellow coworkers. Gallup, Inc. (a global performance-management company responsible for the popular StrengthsFinder phenomenon) echoed this with the "State of the American Workplace" research conducted in 2012. Found in their report is the fact that when we work with unpleasant people we lack closeness with our coworkers. This can reduce our workplace satisfaction by 50 percent. Simply put, your coworkers want to be "actively connected to their larger team."[20] It

---

[20] "State of the American Workplace: Employee Engagement Insights for U.S. Business Leaders," Gallup, Inc. (2013): 28.

is so simple to invite a coworker to lunch, have a conversation with them about their weekend, or suggest a little camaraderie-making at the beginning of a meeting. It truly takes so little to inspire and infect.

I KNOW THEM.

Of the many people you have worked with throughout your career, who did you simply enjoy being around and who made you believe you could do more and be more? These are the people who possess Generate G Factor. Write their names below and take time to identify how they did it.

Name:

How they generated was:

Name:

How they generated was:

Name:

How they generated was:

Name:

How they generated was:

Name:

How they generated was:

CHAPTER SEVEN

GENIUS:
Demonstrate talent and intelligence.

"Talent hits a target no one else can hit; Genius hits a target no one else can see." Arthur Schopenhauer

TRUE STORY. I SWEAR IT.

There have been many people in my life who I consider "intelligent," just as I am sure there have been in yours. Although, the meaning of the word can seem a bit ambiguous. *Merriam-Webster* defines intelligence as "the ability to learn or understand things."[21] In my opinion, realizing and admitting when one does not readily have the intelligence needed for a given situation is talent. Both describe Beth.

---

[21] www.m-w.com

Beth and I haven't ever been employed by the same company; however, she has worked in roles in two organizations in which she hired me for my consulting and training services. Some of the projects I have been hired to do required me to work closely with Beth from initial meeting with a client, to designing a training program, to developing curriculum, to facilitating the program. She likes to tell potential clients she is the task person and I am the people person. I disagree. She has far more talent than just churning out tasks.

Beth doesn't know everything about anything nor does she pretend she does. She completely understands even the most genius of geniuses aren't versed in everything. She openly admits when she doesn't know whatever someone in her position is expected to know. What makes her a genius is she knows *how* to get the information.

Over and over I have witnessed Beth exhibit Genius G Factor with both talent and intelligence.

- Reading books to gather broader and deeper knowledge. This is not only to learn more, but it is also to confirm what is already known to ensure her customers are getting valuable information.
- Tapping in to people who possess strengths she does not. Knowing you are not all things to

everyone is a good career move. She surrounds herself with people who complement her, not compliment her. True Genius G Factor.

- Making connections between theory and the real world. The ability to draw a link between what research shows and how it applies to employers and employees alike. For example, recognizing when meeting with a client that the client is in the resist phase of change and what they need to be able to move through the remaining phases.

- Being a problem finder first and then a problem solver. When meeting with potential clients, they will often identify a solution to address their issue ... except the solution doesn't address the real issue. Beth picks up on this.

- Deciphering useful information from useless information. This trait of genius relates to the last one. She can focus on what needs to be explored to determine the real problem. This talent enables her to solve for the right problem.

- Continuously seeking and finding ways to improve. Working with Beth can sometimes feel as if one is just not doing enough; however, understanding her genius, her true talent and intelligence, is simply knowing and seeking new and better ways to do things. In other words, constant movement toward excellence.

If you were to ask Beth about her Genius G Factor, she would likely brush it off in embarrassment, and because she is continuously on a journey of growth, perhaps she doesn't see her own genius.

EXCUSES PEOPLE USE.

The many faces of genius are usurped by what society deems as genius. Many people I know have bought into the idea that although they are talented, they are not intelligent. I hear this excuse all the time:

"I ain't no Einstein."

Guess what? Few people are. Look around you and ask yourself if the only people you consider having talent and intelligence are Einsteins. Yeah, that's what I thought. You don't have to be Einstein to be a genius. Besides, you likely have better hair than Einstein so that's a plus.

"My IQ isn't that high."

Do you know how many people in the world have a genius IQ? First, a genius IQ requires a score of approximately 140 or higher on the Stanford-Binet Intelligence

Scale. Second, depending on the source, only 1 to 2 percent of the people in the world are considered to have a genius IQ ranking. Do you actually believe only 1 to 2 percent of the world's people are talented and intelligent?

> "You won't believe how many stupid things I do."

Good for you. You are completely normal. Every single human being has moments they can consider to be not their finest. (Which gets me thinking about another idea for a book. Thanks for the idea.)

> "I wasn't ever the smartest kid in the class."

Shhhh. Now, this is just silly. Only one kid in the class gets to be the smartest kid in the class. Does this mean everyone else in the classroom is not talented? Intelligent? Of course not.

The real point here is Genius G Factor isn't defined by your IQ, your book smarts, or your street smarts. So, if you are struggling at all with this, let go of your preconceived idea of what being a genius is and read on.

IT AIN'T JUST HOT AIR.

Intelligence does not produce only one kind of talent; therefore, it makes sense that different talents require different types of intelligences. Think of it this way, an athlete who excels at jumping high or far may be the star of her high school team or a gold medalist in the Olympics (although this takes a great deal of training as well, so let's not discount that). Maybe upon winning a competition she is interviewed by the local TV station, but finds herself searching for words and thoughts to articulate a sentence. Then there is the professional orator who motivates audiences of thousands with inflection, powerful language, and emotion yet struggles to run on a treadmill even though he works out regularly. Perhaps using Dr. Howard Gardner's Theory of Multiple Intelligences will clarify what this means.

In 1983 Dr. Gardner published his theory in the book *Frames of Mind: The Theory of Multiple Intelligences*, which introduced a different way of thinking about intelligence. A person can be smart, so to speak, in some things and not as much in others.

Before you use your intelligence to question if a theory from over three decades ago still applies, let me put your mind at ease. Dr. Gardner's developmental psychological theory is still popular today and is taught at the Harvard Graduate School of Education. And although it is most often applied to learning how to effectively teach children and adolescents, it applies to adult genius as well. Reflect and ponder as you read further.

There are people who like to read, use words and language, listen to words, hold conversations, and discuss things with coworkers. These people possess a great deal of **verbal-linguistic intelligence** and enjoy using or making up mnemonic devices to remember important information. They just might use voice inflection to communicate their message too.

There are those who enjoy numbers and tasks in finance, accounting, or math and can easily think in patterns or sequence. These are people naturally gifted with **logical-mathematical intelligence**. They can be good at puzzles for example and can push through the emotional part of their brain to the front lobe responsible for reason and logic.

Before you keep reading, know this from Dr. Gardner: IQ tests test for linguistic and logical-mathematical intelligence; however, the other six intelligences in the Theory of Multiple Intelligences are left out. This is precisely why many people believe they are either void or deficient of intelligence. You may be a person who can closely identify with the intelligences above, which is great. What is even better is all of us possess multiple intelligences, just to differing degrees. In 2016 Gardner presented his theory at the Blackboard's conference. He said, " ... no two people on the planet, not even identical twins have exactly the same profile of intelligences."[22] So, keep reading to learn about more intelligences.

Individuals who can play music by ear, create arrangements in their head, and enjoy rhythms by dancing to them, listening to them, singing along, etc. have **musical intelligence**. People whose intelligence lives in this arena may actually concentrate better while music plays in the background or when tapping their foot to the sound.

People with strong **interpersonal intelligence** may frequently hear from others, "I feel like I can tell you anything and I don't even know you that well." These folks have a talent for understanding others and making them feel comfortable. They are good at reading social situations through others' facial expressions, voice, and gestures.

Self-aware people who understand what they are about, their strengths, their limitations, and what to do to grow professionally are frequently gifted with **intrapersonal intelligence**. They might excel when working

---

[22] Howard Gardner, "Reflections on Multiple Intelligences Theory," *Project Zero* (Harvard Graduate School of Education: Blackboard BbWorld, 2016). youtube.com/watch?v=8N2pnYne0ZA

alone and will continually measure their progress based on the outcomes desired.

A sign of **spatial** intelligence is when someone tells a story and the listener creates pictures in his or her head. These people make sense out of mazes or follow along with a magician's sleight-of-hand trick. They look around and make connections as to why things are placed where they are. A common phrase they might have heard after playing a strategic game of chess is, "Well played, well played."

Individuals who like to keep their bodies in action while at work and experience their work through movement can relate to **bodily-kinesthetic intelligence**. These can be people who have the most productive meetings when they are not sitting around a conference table but are instead walking while they are talking, problem-solving, and making decisions.

What might seem an obscure intelligence is one that uses the neuro networks in the brain to help make value-based decisions—**naturalist intelligence**. People who are naturally gifted with this type of intelligence can be drawn to anything that connects them to nature. This does not mean they need to be forest rangers, zoologists, or botanists, but instead they draw connections between their choices and how they connect with nature.

In any case, the point is, intelligence and talent as the foundation of Genius G Factor is recognizing and owning both what you are not capable of and what makes you naturally awesome.

I KNOW THEM!

Explore who you have crossed paths with throughout your career, or even in your life.

Name:

Examples of their *verbal-linguistic intelligence:*

1.

2.

Name:

Examples of their *logical-mathematical intelligence:*

1.

2.

Name:

Examples of their *musical intelligence:*

1.

2.

Name:

Examples of their *interpersonal intelligence:*

1.

2.

Name:

Examples of their *intrapersonal intelligence:*

1.

2.

Name:

Examples of their *spatial intelligence:*

1.

2.

Name:

Examples of their *bodily-kinesthetic intelligence:*

1.

2.

Name:

Examples of their *naturalist intelligence:*

1.

2.

CHAPTER EIGHT

GRANT:
Give people
(including myself)
permission to make
mistakes.

"If you have the guts to keep making mistakes, your wisdom and intelligence leap forward with huge momentum." Holly Near

TRUE STORY. I SWEAR IT.

How amazing it is to have a boss who has your back when you make a mistake. This is the leadership approach of the best boss I have ever had. His name is Jack, and he was amazing.

Jack made me want to do better, be better, make him proud, and make him look good. I knew my job was to build the ophthalmology practice we worked for. Of course I don't mean in the construction sense. My job was to build relationships with referring optometrists so they would entrust their surgical patients to our eye surgeons.

No, Jack was not an eye surgeon. He was a successful businessman skilled in business development, and he was good at it.

I grew exponentially in my career when I worked for Jack. I understood my job was to build relationships and referrals. This meant meeting with optometrists and their staff around the state of Minnesota, training them on sales techniques, and building trust. Unbeknownst to Jack, he made me want to find additional ways to connect with referring doctors and those who did not yet refer to our practice. Specifically, I remember starting a newsletter to be distributed to optometrists from our "professional relations" department. Jack not only let me, but he encouraged me to try it and see what happened. He did not analyze whether the newsletter would produce X number of referrals. Instead, he supported me in my endeavor and trusted any mistake I made would not be catastrophic. He was right. There weren't any catastrophic mistakes. Did the newsletter change the world of ophthalmology? No. It built some recognition for the practice and strengthened several relationships with referring doctors. The more important outcome in my eyes is it showed me my boss trusted me and would have had my back had I stumbled. The result? I worked harder and better ... for Jack.

He did not make me feel a mistake would be so big it couldn't be fixed. He made me feel growth comes from stretching yourself and taking calculated risks. And when a person stretches him or herself and takes a risk, they fall and sometimes skin their knees so to speak. But once their knees heal, they know better the next time.

It has been over fifteen years since I worked for Jack. I still carry the lessons from working for him with me. I make choices in my business some might consider unorthodox or against the advice of successful global leaders, yet I continue to grow. As I grow, I offer more insight and better advice to my clients. Even better, I can confidently give them permission to make mistakes so they can grow too.

EXCUSES PEOPLE USE.

Oh, the many excuses we use in an attempt to maintain perfection because we think perfection is what is expected of us. I'm sure there are many conflicting thoughts in your head as you read this excuse:

"Mistakes mean I get fired."

Maybe you aren't working for the right employer, because, after all, you are human. Humans make mistakes and if your employer doesn't realize this, you are working for someone who has expectations you can never meet. This is exhausting and you are being set up to fail.

"I'm a perfectionist."

Um, I'd like to say good for you, but I just can't. What a difficult world it is for those attempting to be what they just cannot be. Part of Grant G Factor is allowing yourself to be a human being. Think of it like this. I am all of five feet one inch. There is nothing I can do to be the model minimum height of 5' 8". Let's be real here, folks. I can't, even on my best day when I am standing with great posture and confidence, reach 5' 2", not without heels anyhow. So, why try? Accept the perfectly imperfect you.

"My parents always expected the best from me."

This is because parents want the best for their children. What would you think if they had told you to reach below your potential? When the excuse is reversed, it sounds a bit ridiculous. Now, I'm not advocating you to not be your best, but if you are going about it in a way that hopes for zero mistakes, you are treating yourself in a most unkind and unrealistic way.

> "It's okay for others to make mistakes, but ...."

Wow. How wonderful of you to give latitude to others but to hold yourself to an unachievable standard. Riddle me this: what is the reason for the double standard?

IT AIN'T JUST HOT AIR.

Much research has been conducted on learning and mistakes in the last decade or so. One of the most popular theories is the theory of Carol Dweck: fixed mind-set vs. growth mind-set. Dweck's theory is people with fixed mind-set believe their intelligence is static and mistakes are a result of their limitations; therefore, these people tend to give up easily. On the other hand, people with growth mind-set believe their intelligence will increase and expand when they make mistakes because they learn how to do things better and differently through reflection and the feedback they receive.

Dr. Jason Moser, associate professor at Michigan State University, conducted a study with four other researchers—Hans Schroeder, Carrie Heeter, Tim

Moran, and Yu-Hao Lee—on how brains act when mistakes are made. They also found it depends on mind-set.

> ... growth mind-set is associated with heightened awareness of and attention to errors .... Overall, the current findings shed new light on the neural underpinnings of growth mind-sets and their links to adaptive responses to mistakes and have important implications for academic and occupational performance.[23]

Studies in the medical field on the types of associations made during learning and the effects associations have on decision-making have also been completed. In a 2011 study, Downar, Bhatt, and Montague used functional magnetic resonance imaging (fMRI) with thirty-five experienced physicians while observing them in virtual patient interactions. The physicians had to choose between two treatments for the patient during the interactions. The purpose of the fMRI, along with behavior observation, was to determine differences between high-performance and low-performance. The study showed, "High performers learned from both

---

[23] Jason S. Moser, Hans S. Schroeder, Carrie Heeter, Tim P. Moran, and Yu-Hao Lee, "Mind Your Errors: Evidence for a neural mechanism linking mind-set to adaptive posterror adjustments," *Psychological Science* 22, no 12 (2011): 1484–1489.

successes and failures, and made smaller rule adjustments after feedback. Conversely, low performers learned disproportionately from successes, and made larger rule adjustments. Nearly half of the physicians performed at chance levels or worse, even after 64 training encounters."[24]

In other words, high-performing physicians learned as much from their failures as from their successes. Conversely, low-performing physicians learned more from successes than from failures. This is important for obvious reasons—as a patient, we want our doctors to learn from their mistakes. Right?

To drive home the point that Grant G Factor is useful, let's look at a couple inventions that are the results of mistakes and think about how life would be different without them.

Chocolate chip cookies. Mmmmm. Have you heard of Ruth Wakefield? Likely not; however, you will be thankful for her as you continue to read. Ruth and her husband owned and ran a lodge named Toll House Inn in the 1930s. On a non-specific day, she was making chocolate cookies for their guests and realized she was out of baker's chocolate. To improvise, Ruth broke a

---

[24] Jonathan Downar, Meghana Bhatt, and P. Read Montague, "Neural Correlates of Effective Learning in Experienced Medical Decision Makers," *PLos ONE* 6, no. 11 (2011). http://dx.doi.org/10.1371/journal.pone.0027768

chocolate bar into pieces and mixed the pieces into the dough, placed them in the oven and waited for the chocolate pieces to melt. To her surprise, they didn't melt. This was the birth of chocolate chip cookies. What a delicious mistake. (A sincere thank-you to Ruth from me personally.)

Next, in almost every work desk and every supply closet we can find the beloved Post-it Note. Just as the chocolate chip cookie, Post-it Notes were born out of a mistake.

In the late 1960s, Dr. Spencer Silver, employed as a scientist and researcher at 3M, created a new adhesive that didn't have a lot of sticking power. The adhesive didn't leave behind residue, but it also wasn't very strong. So, it sat. Several years later a coworker of Silver's, Art Fry, remembered Silver talking once upon a time about this seemingly useless adhesive. Fry's mind began to churn. He thought perhaps applying this adhesive to his ever-falling-out-of-the-hymnal-pieces-of-paper used to mark songs would serve as a stable, yet removable, bookmark. Fry was right. (Perhaps you have even used a version of a Post-it Note to mark the pages of this book.)

I KNOW THEM!

Think about the people in your life who have been good at making mistakes and moving forward. Then note how they used Grant G Factor to allow themselves to push on.

Name:

How they granted was:

Name:

How they granted was:

Name:

How they granted was:

Name:

How they granted was:

Name:

How they granted was:

CHAPTER NINE

GATHER:
Surround myself with others who ooze G Factor.

"As the saying goes that a man is known by the company he keeps. Good company can make a man whereas bad company can ruin him." Sam Veda

MY RESEARCH DIDN'T SEEK to support or confirm Gather G Factor, because I honestly don't believe this G Factor needed validation. Why, you wonder? Think about these phrases:

- You are what you eat.
- You become what you think.
- You become who you associate with.

Essentially, these phrases are saying your habits, behaviors, and people in your life will directly impact the person you are, and I agree.

TRUE STORY. I SWEAR IT.

Throughout my career, I have consistently and constantly surrounded myself with others who ooze G Factor. Stories of these people have been scattered throughout this book, so you have, in some way, met several of them. If you feel like you don't know who I am talking about, you have likely skipped a few chapters in effort to seek out how you can get started on growing your G Factor. I get it. I'm anxious for you too. No worries by the way ... you own the book and can go back when you feel inclined.

EXCUSES PEOPLE USE.

Gather G Factor is where an individual has a lot of power, but sometimes lives his life with a victim mentality, which keeps him connected to others who are not the healthiest. People who have not successfully engaged their Gather G Factor might use some of the excuses below.

> "I don't get to pick who I work with."

Yes, this is true. Everyone has had to work with people who are negative, unpleasant, bossy, lazy, and so on. The part of the statement above that is dangerous is, without maybe realizing it, we expose ourselves to such people when we don't have to. We can sometimes choose the amount of exposure we have to these people. And remember, when we make the choice to act positively, many people naturally return the positivity.

> "I can't fire my boss."

Again, this is true. But your boss is not the only person you interact with at work. If your boss is especially challenging to work for, it is especially important to surround yourself with others who ooze G Factor.

> "I can't quit my job because I don't like the people I work with. I need the money."

I agree. *Don't* quit your job. Think deeply and honestly about the people you work with. Every workplace has someone who oozes G Factor and you need to find them. If you are still thinking, "Not at my company," I encourage you to look deep inside yourself and ask if the reason you don't see them is because you are the one who is deficient in G Factor and are repelling others.

I know. Ouch. Though it had to be said.

IT AIN'T JUST HOT AIR.

Research on how we are influenced by others has existed for decades. Irving Janis's groupthink, Herbert

Kelman's social influence, and Leon Festinger's cognitive dissonance theories serve to describe just a few of these theories.

Perhaps most applicable to G Factor is Festinger's theory. Cognitive dissonance is the "feeling of discomfort resulting from inconsistent attitudes, thoughts, and behaviors,"[25] and it can work for you or against you when it comes to your G Factor. People will try to reduce discomfort by adapting or conforming to what is happening around them. For example, think back to being a child and doing or saying something you didn't feel was who you were, but everyone else was doing or saying it, so you did too. You see, if the people you spend time with repel others through their behavior, it is easy to fall victim to adopting the same behaviors. The reverse is then true. If the people you spend time with get others to gravitate to them because their G Factor is high, you will likely learn and exhibit similar G Factor behaviors to reduce the discomfort of not being like them.

Prior to Festinger's work, psychologist Kurt Lewin spun the psychological community on its heels in 1936 when he asserted a person's *behavior* is a *function* of their *environment*. Your environment is filled with

---

[25] Richard West, and Lynn H. Turner, *Introducing Communication Theory: Analysis and Application* (New York: McGraw-Hill 2010), 113.

people—some with gravitational pull and others who repel. Think of it like a math equation.

B=f(P,E)

Your behavior is largely influenced by the people in your environment and by the environment itself. If your environment is filled with people who have negative, stagnant, selfish, unhappy, judgmental, and lazy behaviors and dispositions, you can expect your behaviors to function conversely to those with G Factor. So, you've got to change what you can control in your environment if you want to grow your G Factor.

An additional theory to consider regarding influence in the workplace is interdependence theory by Harold Kelley and John Thibaut. Essentially, if the rewards are high enough and the costs are low enough, we will become closer to another person. Our closeness to this person produces behaviors of collaboration and meeting their expectations—negative or positive.

I KNOW THEM!

Thinking of the people who work at your organization, answer the questions below.

1) Who is respected?

2) Who stands out as a leader even though they are not in a formal leadership role?

3) Who makes me feel good about my contributions?

4) Who makes me laugh?

5) Who is in tune with what others need to do their work and to feel good at work?

6) Who is good at supporting others and helping people problem solve for themselves?

7) Who lights up the room when they walk into it?

8) Who knows a lot and isn't afraid to admit it and find an answer when they don't?

9) Who takes ownership when they fall short or mess up?

10) Who encourages others after they fall short or mess up?

CHAPTER TEN

HOW TO GROW MY G FACTOR

GROWING MY GRATITUDE G FACTOR: Show my appreciation. (four weeks)

STEP 1. Check all ideas you like.

- ☐ Let others know how their help is important or has contributed to my success.
- ☐ Tell my boss one thing he or she has done to support me.
- ☐ Find someone I interact with every so often and decide what he or she has done to make my job easier.
- ☐ When I think it, write it down and pass it on.
- ☐ Say "please" and "thank you."
- ☐ Tell the person who sits closest to me something he did that makes a difference in how we work together.
- ☐ Leave a treat with a note.

- ☐ Have a conversation with myself about why I appreciate myself.
- ☐ Email a thank-you to someone and carbon copy it to her boss.
- ☐ Choose one person and write down ten reasons I appreciate him. Pick five and write one per sticky note. Leave one at his desk daily for one week.
- ☐ Kitschy treats and phrases:
  - ☐ Thank you for your hard work during the GRIND. (coffee)
  - ☐ You are on FIRE! (Dentyne Fire gum)
  - ☐ You are EXTRAordinary. (Extra gum)
  - ☐ Thank you for the EXTRA effort. (Extra gum)
  - ☐ Thanks a LATTE. (instant latte packet)
  - ☐ You are the BALM! (lip balm)
  - ☐ MOUNDS of thanks. (Mounds candy bar)
  - ☐ Have I told you REESEntly your work is outstanding? (Reese's Peanut Butter Cup)
  - ☐ Have I told you "thank you" REESEntly? (Reese's Peanut Butter Cup)
  - ☐ Have I told you lately you are SOUPer? (soup packet)
  - ☐ You are o-FISH-ally awesome. (Swedish Fish)
  - ☐ A NUGGET of thanks. (Hershey's Nuggets)
  - ☐ Your effort MENTOS much. (Mentos)

STEP 2: Choose one item per week from the previous list (or make up some of your own) and write out your four-week action plan.

WEEK 1

The *first* person I will show appreciation to is:

I will show my gratitude before:

    (day of week) _____,

    (month)_____

    (day)_____,

    (year)_____.

I am **grateful** for

and will show appreciation by

The *second* person I will show appreciation to is:

I will show my gratitude before:

    day of week) _____,

    (month)_____

    (day)_____,

    (year)_____.

I am **grateful** for

and will show appreciation by

WEEK 2

The *first* person I will show appreciation to is:

I will show my gratitude before:
    (day of week) _____,
    (month)_____
    (day)_____,
    (year)_____.

I am **grateful** for

and will show appreciation by

The *second* person I will show appreciation to is:

I will show my gratitude before:
    day of week) _____,
    (month)_____
    (day)_____,
    (year)_____.

I am **grateful** for

and will show appreciation by

WEEK 3

The *first* person I will show appreciation to is:

I will show my gratitude before:
    (day of week) _____,
    (month)_____
    (day)_____,
    (year)_____.

I am **grateful** for

and will show appreciation by

The *second* person I will show appreciation to is:

I will show my gratitude before:
    day of week) _____,
    (month)_____
    (day)_____,
    (year)_____.

I am **grateful** for

and will show appreciation by

WEEK 4

The *first* person I will show appreciation to is:

I will show my gratitude before:
    (day of week) _____,
    (month)_____
    (day)_____,
    (year)_____.

I am **grateful** for

and will show appreciation by

The *second* person I will show appreciation to is:

I will show my gratitude before:
    day of week) _____,
    (month)_____
    (day)_____,
    (year)_____.

I am **grateful** for

and will show appreciation by.

STEP 3. Reflection

I know I have grown my Gratitude G Factor because

_____

_____

_____

GROWING MY GOOD-HUMORED G FACTOR:
Laugh and don't take myself too seriously. (one week)

STEP 1. Check all ideas you like.
- ☐ Learn to tell a joke.
- ☐ Learn to take a joke.
- ☐ Stop by the cubicles of my coworkers, flash a huge smile, and say "good morning."
- ☐ Laugh when I make a mistake (unless it is catastrophic).
- ☐ Share a funny story with a coworker.
- ☐ Find out what is so funny when other people are laughing.
- ☐ Smile.
- ☐ Take a laughter yoga class.
- ☐ Make a list of funny things I have done.
- ☐ Do a cartwheel when walking down a sidewalk (if your body is up to it).
- ☐ When I do something embarrassing, don't try to cover it up.
- ☐ Ask myself, "In five years from now, will this matter?"
- ☐ Take time off.
- ☐ Watch wiener dog races.
- ☐ Whistle (if you can).
- ☐ Dress up for Halloween.

- ☐ Create a rubber chicken award for the person who does the funniest thing in weekly meetings.
- ☐ Dance ... when everyone is watching.
- ☐ Color my hair a bright color.
- ☐ Ask myself, "What can I learn?"

STEP 2: Choose one item from the list above (or make up one of your own) and write out your Day 1 action plan and then revise daily.

Day 1: _____ (date)

I will do: _____.

    End-of-day reflection:

        One thing I did well is

        _____.

        One thing I can do better is

        _____.

Day 2: _____

I will do (revised from Day 1 reflection) _____

_____.

    End-of-day reflection:

        One thing I did well is

        _____.

        One thing I can do better is

        _____.

Day 3: _____

I will do (revised from Day 2 reflection) _____.
    End-of-day reflection:
        One thing I did well is

        _____.

        One thing I can do better is

        _____.

Day 4: _____

I will do (revised from Day 3 reflection) _____

_____.

    End-of-day reflection:
        One thing I did well is

        _____.

        One thing I can do better is

        _____.

Day 5: _____

I will do (revised from Day 4 reflection) _____

_____.

    End-of-day reflection:
        One thing I did well is

        _____.

        One thing I can do better is

        _____.

STEP 3. Reflection

I know I have grown my Good-humored G Factor because

_____

_____

_____

GROWING MY GENEROSITY G FACTOR:
Show kindness and concern. (two weeks)

STEP 1. Check all ideas you like.
- ☐ Welcome the newest employee in person and ask if he has questions.
- ☐ When a coworker has a tough day, ask her if she wants to talk.
- ☐ Don't participate in gossip and ask others not to.
- ☐ Offer to help a coworker who is stressed.
- ☐ Invite a coworker for a lunchtime walk if he is having a challenging day.
- ☐ Initiate a real conversation: ask questions and listen.
- ☐ Bring someone a cup of coffee.
- ☐ Offer to heat up someone's lunch and have it ready when she enters the lunchroom.
- ☐ Make a list of people who annoy me; then write down one positive thing about each of them.
- ☐ Donate vacation time if my company allows it.
- ☐ Start a collection for a coworker in need (e.g., food, money, etc.).
- ☐ Ask my coworkers what they need from me.
- ☐ Be sensitive to others' timelines.
- ☐ If I can't say it to their faces, don't say it.
- ☐ Hold a door open.
- ☐ Pull out a chair for a coworker (not out from underneath him by the way).

- ☐ Grab someone a napkin.
- ☐ Make a pot of coffee.
- ☐ Write a note to let a coworker know she is on my mind.
- ☐ Take on a task a coworker doesn't like.

STEP 2: Choose up to ten items from the list above (or make up some of your own) and write out your two-week action plan AND revisit daily to capture coworker reactions in writing.

Day 1: _____

I will do: _____.

The reaction was: _____.

Day 2: _____

I will do: _____.

The reaction was: _____.

Day 3: _____

I will do: _____.

The reaction was: _____.

Day 4: _____

I will do: _____.

The reaction was: _____.

Day 5: _____

I will do: _____.

The reaction was: _____.

Day 6: _____

I will do: _____.

The reaction was: _____.

Day 7: _____

I will do: _____.

The reaction was: _____.

Day 8: _____

I will do: _____.

The reaction was: _____.

Day 9: _____

I will do: _____.

The reaction was: _____.

Day 10: _____

I will do: _____.

The reaction was: _____.

STEP 3. Reflection

I know I have grown my Generosity G Factor because

_____

_____

_____

GROWING MY GUIDE G FACTOR: Coach instead of direct. (six weeks)

STEP 1. Check all ideas you like.

- ☐ Do more asking and less telling.
- ☐ Be a thinking partner.
- ☐ Listen.
- ☐ Show interest.
- ☐ Be objective.
- ☐ Check in on progress.
- ☐ Look for "coaching moments" (unplanned opportunities to coach).
- ☐ Hold others accountable without coming off punitive.
- ☐ Be positive.
- ☐ Be honest.
- ☐ Delegate and let go.
- ☐ Avoid criticizing, being negative, and judging.
- ☐ Be the role model.
- ☐ Use an informal approach when giving input.
- ☐ Encourage others to develop their own solutions.
- ☐ Ask for coaching training.
- ☐ Read one of the sources listed under chapter five in the Resources section.

STEP 2: Choose two ideas from the previous list (or make up two of your own) and write out your six-week action plan.

*Note: As you read through the weekly steps to grow your Guide G Factor you may wonder why the end goal is to increase coaching behavior by only 50 percent. The reason is all job roles require some amount of directing. If you believe your role requires less than 50 percent directing, continue the exercise for an additional three weeks to achieve an outcome of 25 percent directing and 75 percent coaching.

IDEA ONE _____

Week 1 Goal: awareness. For thirty minutes per day, track how many times you do the opposite of idea one by documenting each time with a hashmark. (For example, if you chose "do more asking than telling," record one hashmark for each time you find yourself unnecessarily telling someone what to do or how to do it.)

_____

_____

_____

Week 2 Goal: increase the number of times you use the chosen coaching behavior by 25 percent. Again, for thirty minutes per day track how many times you do the opposite of idea one by documenting with hashmarks.

_____

_____

_____

- At the end of the week, compare week 1 and week 2 results. Do you have 25 percent fewer hashmarks?

Week 3 Goal: increase the number of times you use the chosen coaching behavior by an additional 25 percent. Again, for thirty minutes per day track how many times you do the opposite of idea one by documenting with hashmarks.

_____

_____

_____

- At the end of the week, compare week 2 and week 3 results. Do you have 25 percent fewer hashmarks?

IDEA TWO _____

Week 4 Goal: awareness. For thirty minutes per day, track how many times you do the opposite of idea one by documenting each time with a hashmark. (For example, if you chose "do more asking than telling," record one hashmark for each time you find yourself unnecessarily telling someone what to do or how to do it.)

_____

_____

_____

Week 5 Goal: increase the number of times you use the chosen coaching behavior by 25 percent. Again, for thirty minutes per day track how many times you do the opposite of idea one by documenting with hashmarks.

_____

_____

_____

- At the end of the week, compare week 4 and week 5 results. Do you have 25 percent fewer hashmarks?

Week 6 Goal: increase the number of times you use the chosen coaching behavior by an additional 25 percent. Again, for thirty minutes per day track how many times you do the opposite of idea one by documenting with hashmarks.

_____

_____

_____

- At the end of the week, compare week 5 and week 6 results. Do you have 25 percent fewer hashmarks?

STEP 3. Reflection

I know I have grown my Guide G Factor because

_____

_____

_____

GROWING MY GENERATE G FACTOR: Inspire and be infectious. (two weeks)

STEP 1. Check all ideas you like.

- ☐ Be kind.
- ☐ Be positive.
- ☐ Be forward-thinking.
- ☐ Be respectful.
- ☐ Conduct myself with integrity.
- ☐ Smile.
- ☐ Laugh.
- ☐ Admit it when I screw up.
- ☐ Verbalize another person's good work.
- ☐ Follow through.
- ☐ Encourage others when they do not see their own ability.
- ☐ Do good work.
- ☐ Take others to task when they gossip (respectfully).
- ☐ Don't gossip.
- ☐ Be inventive.
- ☐ Show commitment to my team.
- ☐ Write a thoughtful note.

STEP 2: Put seven ideas you checked above (or some of your own) into daily practice. On your breaks reflect and record the number of times you did each. At the end of the day write down the number of times

you did each in the table below. (The goal for your two-week practice is one hundred.)

Generate G Factor behavior	Day 1	Day 2	Day 3	Day 4	Day 5	Day 6	Day 7	Day 8	Day 9	Day 10	TOTAL
GRAND TOTAL											

STEP 3. Reflection

I know I have grown my Generate G Factor because

_____

_____

_____

GROWING MY GENIUS G FACTOR:
Demonstrate talent and intelligence. (three weeks)

STEP 1. Check all ideas you like.

- ☐ Be a lifelong learner.
- ☐ Learn something new every day.
- ☐ Read more.
- ☐ Ask more questions.
- ☐ Hone my skills.
- ☐ Identify what I am good at and do more of it.
- ☐ Recognize when I need to get more information.
- ☐ Admit it when I don't know.
- ☐ Marry my gut feeling with logic.
- ☐ Learn how the brain mediates conflicting thoughts.
- ☐ Do something that makes me uncomfortable.
- ☐ Stop telling myself I'm not smart.
- ☐ Stand tall and project confidence.
- ☐ Make a list of my talents.

STEP 2: Choose one of the ideas you checked above or an idea of your own and practice it for ten minutes each day.

I will do: _____

_____.

Day 1: Start time_____ End time_____

I have become more talented and intelligent because I can now do or know

_____

Day 2: Start time_____ End time_____

I have become more talented and intelligent because I can now do or know

_____

Day 3: Start time_____ End time_____

I have become more talented and intelligent because I can now do or know

_____

Day 4: Start time_____ End time_____

I have become more talented and intelligent because I can now do or know

_____

Day 5: Start time_____ End time_____

I have become more talented and intelligent because I can now do or know

_____

Day 6: Start time_____ End time_____

I have become more talented and intelligent because I can now do or know

_____

Day 7: Start time_____ **End time**_____
I have become more talented and intelligent because I can now do or know

_____

Day 8: Start time_____ **End time**_____
I have become more talented and intelligent because I can now do or know

_____

Day 9: Start time_____ **End time**_____
I have become more talented and intelligent because I can now do or know

_____

Day 10: Start time_____ **End time**_____
I have become more talented and intelligent because I can now do or know

_____

Day 11: Start time_____ **End time**_____
I have become more talented and intelligent because I can now do or know

_____

Day 12: Start time_____ **End time**_____
I have become more talented and intelligent because I can now do or know

_____

Day 13: Start time_____ End time_____

I have become more talented and intelligent because I
can now do or know

_____

Day 14: Start time_____ End time_____

I have become more talented and intelligent because I
can now do or know

_____

Day 15: Start time_____ End time_____

I have become more talented and intelligent because I
can now do or know

_____

STEP 3. Reflection

I know I have grown my Genius G Factor because

_____

_____

_____

GROWING MY GRANT G FACTOR: Give people (including myself) permission to make mistakes. (two weeks)

STEP 1. Check all ideas you like.

- ☐ Reframe mistakes as
  - ° learning opportunities.
  - ° finding ways not to do things.
  - ° growth.
  - ° simply being human.
  - ° something that is not the end of the world.
- ☐ Be kind to myself.
- ☐ Ask myself, "How impactful is the mistake?"
- ☐ Stop telling myself to be perfect.
- ☐ Stop expecting others to be perfect.
- ☐ Ensure expectations are realistic.
- ☐ Encourage exploration.
- ☐ Recognize no one is perfect.
- ☐ Stop worrying how a mistake will make me look.
- ☐ Change my mind-set.
- ☐ Celebrate accidents.

STEP 2. At the end of the day, choose one mistake you or someone else made. Then choose an idea from above and complete the questions below.

Example for a mistake made by myself:

Mistake: *I gave a presentation to another department and had spelling errors in my PowerPoint presentation.*

Idea chosen from Step 1: *Encourage exploration.*

Apply idea above: *Explore why I did not proof and edit the PowerPoint prior to the presentation.*

Outcome of applying idea above: *I didn't proof and edit because I was overwhelmed with other tasks.*

Permission to make a mistake: *I am still productive and this is not a mistake I frequently make.*

Example for mistake made by someone else.

Mistake: Misquoted a price to a customer.

Idea chosen from Step 1: *Recognize no one is perfect.*

Apply idea above: *It was just a mistake; one I could have easily made early in my career.*

Outcome of applying idea above: *I'm not letting the mistake affect the working relationship with my coworker.*

Permission to make a mistake: *I won't expect others to be perfect.*

Day 1 Mistake: _____.

  Idea chosen from Step 1:

  Apply idea above:

  Outcome of applying idea above:

  Permission to make a mistake:

Day 2 Mistake: _____.

  Idea chosen from Step 1:

  Apply idea above:

  Outcome of applying idea above:

  Permission to make a mistake:

Day 3 Mistake: _____.

  Idea chosen from Step 1:

  Apply idea above:

Outcome of applying idea above:

Permission to make a mistake:

Day 4 Mistake: _____.

Idea chosen from Step 1:

Apply idea above:

Outcome of applying idea above:

Permission to make a mistake:

Day 5 Mistake: _____.

Idea chosen from Step 1:

Apply idea above:

Outcome of applying idea above:

Permission to make a mistake:

Day 6 Mistake: _____.

   Idea chosen from Step 1:

   Apply idea above:

   Outcome of applying idea above:

   Permission to make a mistake:

Day 7 Mistake: _____.

   Idea chosen from Step 1:

   Apply idea above:

   Outcome of applying idea above:

   Permission to make a mistake:

Day 8 Mistake: _____.

   Idea chosen from Step 1:

   Apply idea above:

Outcome of applying idea above:

Permission to make a mistake:

Day 9 Mistake: _____.

Idea chosen from Step 1:

Apply idea above:

Outcome of applying idea above:

Permission to make a mistake:

Day 10 Mistake: _____.

Idea chosen from Step 1:

Apply idea above:

Outcome of applying idea above:

Permission to make a mistake:

STEP 3. Reflection

I know I have grown my Grant G factor because

_____

_____

_____

GROWING MY GATHER G FACTOR: Surround myself with others who ooze G Factor.

- Complete an inventory of who I spend my time with.
- Know who gives me positive energy.
- Know who gives me negative energy.
- Know who robs me of energy.
- Make changes.
- Set up coffee dates.
- Schedule informational interviews.
- Seek out responsibilities on other teams.
- Become the standard.
- Limit exposure to those who lack G Factor.
- Set boundaries.

STEP 1. Brainstorm and evaluate My Equation/Circles of Influence {$B=f(P,E)$} (one to four weeks)

INNER CIRCLE

- People I know well *and*
- have contact with regularly.

(e.g., spouse, friends, some extended family, loyal customers, coworkers in my department)

Which *two* people have the *highest* G Factor?

1.

2.

Which *two* people have the *lowest* G Factor?

1.

2.

MIDDLE CIRCLE

- People I associate with *but*
- do not have a personal relationship with.

(e.g., networking groups, trade associations, PTA/PTO, some coworkers)

Which *two* people have the *highest* G Factor?

1.

2.

Which *two* people have the *lowest* G Factor?

1.

2.

OUTER CIRCLE

- People I see infrequently.
- People who associate with people in my inner or middle circle.
- People I want to get to know.

(e.g., dentist, banker, financial planner, spouse's boss, a friend's client, parents of your children's friends, business owner, president of a volunteer organization)

Which *two* people have the *highest* G Factor?

1.

2.

Which *two* people have the *lowest* G Factor?

1.

2.

STEP 2. Set up a coffee or lunch with one person from my inner circle, middle circle, and outer circle who have high G Factor.

INNER CIRCLE: (Name)_____

_____ _____ __,_____ _____
Day of Week   Month   Date   Year

MIDDLE CIRCLE: (Name)_____

_____ _____ __,_____ _____
Day of Week   Month   Date   Year

OUTER CIRCLE: (Name)_____

_____ _____ __,_____ _____
Day of Week   Month   Date   Year

STEP 3. Determine four questions to ask each person.

INNER CIRCLE: (Name)_____

Q1.

Q2.

Q3.

Q4.

MIDDLE CIRCLE: (Name)_____

Q1.

Q2.

Q3.

Q4.

OUTER CIRCLE: (Name)_____

Q1.

Q2.

Q3.

Q4.

Step 4. Reflection

I know I have grown my Gather G factor because

_____

_____

_____

CHAPTER ELEVEN

I Grew My G Factor, Now What?

FIRST, LET'S CELEBRATE TOGETHER! You have been on an amazing journey of personal and professional growth. Along the way you have likely had some discoveries, some surprises, and some successes. This is exciting for you, and it is exciting for me too. I want to hear about your growth and experiences. Please stop by my website and share your story (www.expressivecct.com/books).

Next, let's revisit each of the G Factors and why they are important for your success.

GRATITUDE: Show my appreciation.

Letting others know we are grateful for their help or contributions promotes loyalty and increases a person's well-being: yours and theirs too.

GOOD-HUMORED: Laugh and don't take myself too seriously.

Having fun and keeping things in perspective with smiles, laughter, cheerfulness, and joy is powerfully positive for you and for others.

GENEROSITY: Show kindness and concern for others.

Doing nice things for others typically brings about human nature's in-kind response and human biology's natural high for you.

GUIDE: Coach instead of direct.

Approaching a person with less telling and more respect provides the motivation they need and increases the likelihood of success for both of you.

GENERATE: Inspire and be infectious.

Identifying what is unique and special about you, then embracing it, owning it, and sharing it with others creates inspiration for you and for others.

GENUIS: Demonstrate talent and intelligence.

Knowing intelligence comes in many forms and which forms we have and don't have is key to maximizing what we focus on and how we tap into others' talents.

GRANT: Give people (including myself) permission to make mistakes.

Making mistakes creates opportunities for growth and allows each of us to become our best without hiding behind embarrassment or shame.

GATHER: Surround myself with others who ooze G Factor.

Knowing we become products of our environment means we need to carefully choose who we are around, because it directly impacts our own G Factor.

Finally, our workplaces are changing all the time, which means the people we interact with change. From project to project, new hire to new hire, and shifting of responsibilities, there are new people we can draw to us or repel. There will always be new people to show gratitude to, to guide, to grant, and so on. But let's not forget about the people who have been there all along. They will need care and feeding too.

If you want to maintain your G Factor it will require daily effort. Think of it like a workout regime. You work out for a while and tone up, lose the desired amount of weight, and achieve your fitness goals. Does this mean you can stop working out? Not if you want to maintain your new level of fitness. G Factor is the same. So, keep at it. Make G Factor your new way of being by growing it each and every day.

References

Chapter Two

Bersin & Associates. What Works Market Brief: Turning Thank You into Performance (June, 2012).

www.ted.com/talks/martin_seligman_on_the_state_of_psychology

www.positivepsychologyprogram.com/founding-fathers

Gratitude Visit. https://www.youtube.com/watch?v=jy LYgR2nDkc

Chapter Three

www.patchadams.org/patch-adams

www.twitter.com/richardbranson

www.virgin.com/richard-branson/toilet-roll-humour-35000-feet

Chapter Four

Robert Bolton and Dorothy Grover Bolton, *People Styles at Work and Beyond: Making Bad Relationships Good and*

Good Relationships Better (New York: Ridge Associates, Inc., 2009).

www.gsb.stanford.edu/insights/psychology-kindness-workplace

David R. Hamilton, *Why Kindness is Good for You* (London: Hay House Publishers, 2010).

David R. Hamilton, *The Contagious Power of Thinking: How Your Thoughts Can Influence the World* (London: Hay House Publishers, 2011).

Chapter Five

Coaching People: Encourage Employees, Listen Actively, Clarify Roles, Adapt Your Style: Expert Solutions for Everyday Challenges (Pocket Mentor Series, Harvard Business School Press, 2006).

www.cpiworld.com/knowledge-center/white-papers/the-power-of-a-coaching-culture-on-organizational-performance

www.forbescustom.com/DiversityPgs/UnityFirst/08.15.11/ResearchShowsImpact.html

www.nzli.co.nz/file/Conference/Presentations/the-power-of-peer-coaching-tools-for-effective-leadership-coaching-groups.pdf

www.workplacepsychology.net/2010/08/28/the-benefits-of-coaching-employees/

Chapter Six

www.businesswire.com/news/home/20151116006254/en/
Zenger-Folkman-Research-Shows-Inspiring-Worth-Effort

www.cleverism.com/motivation-employees-best-way/

www.forbes.com/sites/victorlipman/2014/11/04/what-
motivates-employees-to-go-the-extra-mile-study-offers-
surprising-answer/3/#7344d71175e8

www.nrc-cnrc.gc.ca/eng/careers/behavioural_competen-
cies/mg_inspirational_leadership.html

Chapter Seven

Howard Gardner, *Frames of Mind: The Theory of Multiple Intelligences* (Philadelphia: Basic Books, 2011).

PSIA. Rocky Mountain Division. AASI. (2014) Theory of Multiple Intelligences from Frames of Mind: The Theory of Multiple Intelligences

www.soundpiper.com/mln/mi.htm

Chapter Eight

Carol S. Dweck, *Mindset: The New Psychology of Success* (New York: Random House, 2006).

www.brainpickings.org/2014/01/29/carol-dweck-mindset

www.npr.org/2014/07/26/335402996/an-idea-that-stuck-
how-a-hymnal-bookmark-helped-inspire-the-post-it-note

www.post-it.com/3M/en_US/post-it/contact-us/about-us/

www.ted.com/talks/carol_dweck_the_power_of_believing_that_you_can_improve?language=en

www.women-inventors.com/Ruth-Wakefield

Chapter Nine

Ernest G. Bormann, *Small Group Communication Theory and Practice* (New York: Harper & Row, Publishers, Inc., 1990).

www.britannica.com/biography/Kurt-Lewin

Made in the USA
Coppell, TX
08 September 2023